INTERACTIVE WORKBOOK

WHAT HAPPENS
WHEN WOMEN
SAY *Yes* ^{TO} *God*

LYSA TERKEURST

HARVEST HOUSE PUBLISHERS
EUGENE, OREGON

Cover by Garborg Design Works, Savage, Minnesota

Cover photo © Aspireimages / Inmagine

Published in association with the literary agency of Fedd & Company, Inc., 606 Flamingo Blvd., Austin, TX 78734

WHAT HAPPENS WHEN WOMEN SAY YES TO GOD INTERACTIVE WORKBOOK

Copyright © 2011 by Lysa TerKeurst with Christine M. Anderson

Published by Harvest House Publishers

Eugene, Oregon 97402

www.harvesthousepublishers.com

ISBN 978-0-7369-2894-6 (pbk.)

Printed in the United States of America

20 21 22 23 / VP-NI / 23 22 21 20

CONTENTS

An Invitation to Say Yes

No matter who you are, no matter where you've been, no matter what your current circumstances are, nothing needs to happen to clean you up or to make you more spiritually mature before you start becoming a woman who says yes to God. It can happen today. If God could take the frail and fragile yes I whispered more than 20 years ago and birth this adventure I've been living, it is possible for any woman—including you—to live the great adventure her soul is designed to live.

When a woman says to God, her obedience sets off a chain reaction of divine change—she changes, those around her change, and the world changes. Truly, one person saying yes to God can change the world. I believe that with all my heart. That doesn't mean our obedience will be broadcast on the evening news, but it will start a series of events that could lead many people to experience God. I've seen it happen over and over.

I want you to experience God that way. I want you to know deep down in your bones that He can be so much more than just an item on our good-Christian-girl checklist. God is truly to be experienced in an intimate relationship, and He invites us to encounter Him every day. Will you accept the invitation?

My dear friend, it truly is that simple. Just whisper yes today and watch the adventure unfold.

Lysa TerKeurst

HOW TO USE THIS WORKBOOK

GROUP SIZE

The *What Happens When Women Say Yes to God DVD* is designed to be experienced in a group setting, such as a Bible study, Sunday school class, or any small-group gathering. To ensure everyone has enough time to participate in the discussions, it is recommended that large groups break up into smaller groups of four to six people.

Each participant should have her own interactive workbook, which includes notes for DVD segments, directions for activities and discussion questions, and reading plans and personal studies to deepen learning between sessions. Although the course can be fully experienced with just the DVD and interactive workbook, participants are also encouraged to have a copy of the *What Happens When Women Say Yes to God* book. Reading the book along with the DVD sessions provides even deeper insights that will make the journey richer and more meaningful.

WHAT'S INCLUDED

What Happens When Women Say Yes to God Interactive Workbook includes:

- Six group sessions
- Six personal studies for use between sessions. These include suggested chapter readings from the *What Happens When Women Say Yes to God* book and personal studies that track along with the DVD teaching for group sessions.

TIMING

The time notations—for example, (31 minutes)—indicate the actual time of DVD segments and the suggested times for each activity or discussion. Adhering to the suggested times will enable you to complete each group session in one hour. If you have additional time, you may wish to allow more time for discussion and activities.

FACILITATION

Each group should appoint a facilitator who is responsible for starting the DVD and for keeping track of time during discussions and activities. Facilitators may also read questions aloud and monitor discussions, prompting participants to respond and assuring that everyone has the opportunity to participate.

PERSONAL STUDY

Maximize the impact of the course between sessions with additional reading in the *What Happens When Women Say Yes to God* book and a personal study on the theme of the session for that week. Setting aside additional time between sessions for reading and personal study will enable you to complete the book and the studies by the end of the course.

So are you ready to begin this journey of learning to say yes to God? It is sure to be an adventure not quickly forgotten.

The Power of One
Comfortable vs. Comfort-able

Group Study

WELCOME!

Welcome to Session 1 of the *What Happens When Women Say Yes to God DVD*. If this is your first time together as a group, take a moment to introduce yourselves to one another before watching the DVD. Then let's get started!

DVD: *The Power of One* (31 Minutes)

As you watch the DVD, use the notes below to follow along or to add your own notes about anything that stands out to you.

NOTES

We all have a story, a history.

His + story = how God weaves in and out of our lives.

Lysa's story
- Rejection, abandonment, abuse, loss
- Searching for love and significance
- A note from a woman who listened to God, even when it didn't make any sense at all.
- "'For I know the plans I have for you,' declares the LORD, 'plans to prosper you and not to harm you, plans to give you hope and a future'" (Jeremiah 29:11 NIV).

Luke 17: The story of the ten lepers. "I know what it feels like to have leprosy of the soul."

When the Messiah touches our mess, it becomes our message to the world.

Nine lepers had their mess touched by the Messiah, but only one turned it into a message.

God's goal isn't to make us comfortable. His goal is to make us comfort-*able*—able to take the comfort we have received and give it to others.

"Praise be to the God and Father of our Lord Jesus Christ, the Father of compassion and the God of all comfort, who comforts us in all our troubles, so that we can comfort those in any trouble with the comfort we ourselves have received from God" (2 Corinthians 1:3-4 NIV).

This Week's Assignment

Say yes to God when you come across someone who needs to hear some part of your story.

When a woman says yes to God, the world is changed.

GROUP DISCUSSION: *The Power of One* (5 Minutes)

Take a few minutes to talk about what you just watched.

1. What part of the teaching had the most impact on you?

2. How do you respond to the idea that we all have a story?

INDIVIDUAL ACTIVITY: *What's My Story?* (3 Minutes)

Complete this activity on your own.

1. "We may not have a movie made of our life," Lysa says, "but we all live out some kind of story." If someone were to make a movie of your life, which of the phrases below might a movie reviewer or viewer use to describe your story? In other words, how might someone complete this sentence: "This story is about…" (Check all that apply.)

___ An epic journey	___ An identity crisis
___ The loss of innocence	___ Hoping against hope
___ Gains and losses	___ A battle against injustice
___ Restoration	___ Severe mercies
___ Humble beginnings	___ Growing pains
___ Sacrifices and rewards	___ The heartbreak of betrayal
___ Battles won and lost	___ A fear of failure
___ A fall from grace	___ A dream come true
___ Villains and heroes	___ Facing darkness
___ A big trick	✓ Beauty from ashes
___ Rebirth	___ Going against the odds
___ Pride and downfall	___ Hilarity and heartbreak
___ Unanswered questions	___ Learning the hard way
___ A life-and-death struggle	___ A never-ending battle
___ Grace	___ Risk and reward
___ Overcoming the past	___ A search for love and significance
___ Mystery and beauty	___ Other: _____
___ Reconciliation	

2. Most stories have a thread or theme that weaves in and out from beginning to end. Reviewing the phrases you checked above, which do you think might come closest to describing the overall theme of your life's story? Circle your top two or three choices.

GROUP DISCUSSION: *What's My Story?* (7 Minutes)

1. Is it easy or difficult for you to think of your life as a story? Why?

2. If you feel comfortable doing so, share the two or three phrases you circled to describe the overall theme of your story. What is it about these phrases that resonates most with you?

GROUP DISCUSSION: *The Story of the Ten Lepers* (12 Minutes)

1. Read Luke 17:11-19 aloud.

2. The ten lepers are what some would have unjustifiably deemed as "throwaway people"— they are wounded, unable to alleviate their own suffering, shunned by the people they love, and cut off from everything familiar to them. And yet, despite the fact that their lives are a tragic mess, they are not without hope. They believe Jesus can heal them, and they cry out to Him for mercy (verse 13 NKJV).

   • In what ways, if any, do you relate to the experience of the ten lepers? For example, Lysa noted she knew what it felt like to have "leprosy of the soul."

   • When your life is difficult and messy, how do your circumstances impact your relationship with God? Are you able to remain hopeful, or do you struggle to believe God will hear your cries and have mercy on you?

3. When they are healed, nine of the ten lepers are content to do their duty—present themselves to the priests—and then quietly put their disgraceful and messy lives behind them. But one leper practically shouts his story from the rooftops. His praises are loud and his gratitude dramatic as he throws himself at Jesus' feet in an act of worship (verses 15-16).

   • What do you think might have prevented the nine lepers from returning to give thanks and from making their story more public?

   • When it comes to the messiness of your own life, do you tend to be more like the nine lepers, wanting to put your difficult past quietly behind you? Or are you more like the one leper, eager to tell your story as an act of gratitude and worship?

4. All ten lepers are healed, but the one leper who returns also receives something more, a deeper healing. Jesus commends him and says, "Your faith has made you well" (verse 19 NIV). This statement can also be translated as, "Your faith has restored you" (AMP). What deeper healing do you think we might receive from God when we allow our mess to become our message to others?

INDIVIDUAL ACTIVITY: *What I Want to Remember* (2 Minutes)

Complete this activity on your own.

1. Briefly review any notes you took.

2. In the space below, write down the most significant thing you gained in this session—from the teaching, activities, or discussions.

What I want to remember from this session…

He blessed the one even even further. His spirit healed.
God loves the grateful heart. "What would our lives - our kids (Sarah) look like if we didn't
have faith? to depend on because of the challenges we've faced w/ Sarah.
There's purpose in our pain.

CLOSING PRAYER

Close your time together with prayer.

ON YOUR OWN

After each group session, you'll have a chance to do some additional study and reflection on your own. This includes reading chapters from the *What Happens When Women Say Yes to God* book and completing a personal study on the theme of that week's group session. Setting aside additional time for reading and study between sessions deepens the experience of the course and will help to make your journey richer and even more meaningful.

PERSONAL STUDY

READ AND REFLECT

Read chapter 1 of *What Happens When Women Say Yes to God*. If you want to dig a little deeper, use a notepad or journal to work through the Bible study at the end of the chapter. Use the space below to note any insights or questions you want to bring to the next group session.

MY STORY + GOD'S STORY = *HI*STORY

Saying yes begins with you—your story. The one that only you can tell. If it has some rough patches in it, you can allow them to work for you, not against you. You can't change those aspects of your past, but you can change whether or not you allow God to use them for harm or for good. In fact, those rough patches may be some of your best qualifications when it comes to saying yes to God. That's because God is in the change and transformation business—and if He's changed your life, then you can be sure He wants to use your story to help change someone else's life.

> I love the word "history" because...if we break
> that word up we see that it means "His story."
> It's how God weaves in and out of our lives.
>
> *What Happens When Women Say Yes to God DVD*

1. God is always at work in our lives, even when we aren't aware of it. In fact, the Bible says God knows us even before we are conceived! (Jeremiah 1:5). Generally speaking, is it easy or difficult for you to recognize God's work in your life? Circle the number below that best describes your response.

1	2	3	4	5
Very difficult	Fairly difficult	Sometimes difficult, sometimes easy	Fairly easy	Very easy

If God is always at work in our lives—creating "His story"—how might it change the way you view the difficult times you've experienced?

God's goal isn't to make us comfortable. His goal is to make us comfort-*able*—able to take the comfort we have received and give it to others.

What Happens When Women Say Yes to God DVD

---

2. The apostle Paul describes how comfort is a gift that keeps on giving:

Praise be to the God and Father of our Lord Jesus Christ, the Father of compassion and the God of all comfort, who comforts us in all our troubles, so that we can comfort those in any trouble with the comfort we ourselves have received from God (2 Corinthians 1:3-4 NIV).

- Recall an experience in which you received comfort from someone, recently or in the past. What was it that this person did or said (or did *not* do or say) that was especially comforting to you?

- At the time, did you recognize the comfort you received as God's comfort, delivered to you through the person who helped you? Why or why not?

- If we can receive comfort directly from God, why do you think God also wants us to comfort others in the same way we have been comforted?

Our mess is a perfect match for the Messiah. And when the Messiah touches our mess, it's then supposed to become our message to the world.

What Happens When Women Say Yes to God DVD

---

3. In order to share your story as a way of reaching out and comforting others, you first have to know what your story is! Use the guidelines on pages 17–19 to help you think through your life experiences and how God has made "His story" alive in your story.

MY MESSES

What are the messes in your life story? These might be difficult things that happened through no fault of your own or mistakes you've made that cause you to feel shame or embarrassment. If you had a relatively uneventful or happy childhood, these messes might just be insecurities or misperceptions about God's love. We all have imperfect gaps in our lives. So even if your circumstances don't seem dramatic, you still have ways Jesus has woven "His story" into your story. Use the space below to write down three to five events or experiences that come to mind.

Lysa's examples: *A troubled childhood that included rejection and abandonment by her father, the divorce of her parents, childhood abuse by a family friend, and feeling as though she were a throwaway person. Painful experiences in young adulthood that included the death of her baby sister, rejecting God, searching for love and significance in the world, an abortion, emotional pain, and depression.*

MY MESSIAH MOMENTS

What are the Messiah moments in your life story? These might be times when God intervened to demonstrate His love and care for you, provide for you, or help you to experience healing.

Lysa's examples: *Crying out to God for help from the depths of emotional pain and depression, receiving a note from her Bible friend that included a verse of hope (Jeremiah 29:11), experiencing God's love and forgiveness, and discovering she was not a throwaway person but a child of God, saying yes to God.*

MY MESSAGES

What might be some of the potential messages of your life story? In other words, how might you comfort others with the same comfort you have received from God?

Remember, telling your life story isn't just about regurgitating past circumstances. It's about telling others how God helped you so they can be encouraged and believe that God can help them too.

Lysa's example: *Helping others to see that they are not throwaway people—they are beloved children of God.*

4. Take a moment to review what you wrote down for question 3 on pages 17-19—your messes, Messiah moments, and messages. To help clarify your story and make it easier to share with others, choose one of the experiences you wrote down as a mess and use it as the focus for the following exercise.

   After reviewing the example below, use the chart on page 21 to briefly describe the three components of your experience—mess, Messiah moment, and message. Write them just as you might say them to someone in conversation. Then reread your responses and summarize each one in a sentence.

EXAMPLE

MY MESS What Was Wrong in My Life	MY MESSIAH MOMENT How Jesus Met Me in My Mess	MY MESSAGE How I Can Use My Story to Comfort Others
After painful losses early in life, I rejected God and tried to find love and significance in the world. I had an abortion and experienced deep pain and depression. I felt that I was a throwaway person.	*On the very day my baby would have been due, when the pain was so deep I wanted to die, I received a note from a friend that gave me hope. I discovered I was not a throwaway person but a beloved child of God.*	*No matter what pain and mistakes are in your past, you are not a throwaway person. You are a beloved child of God.*
One-sentence summary: *I felt that I was a throwaway person.*	**One-sentence summary:** *I discovered I was not a throwaway person but a beloved child of God.*	**One-sentence summary:** *You are not a throwaway person. You are a beloved child of God.*

MY MESS What Was Wrong in My Life	MY MESSIAH MOMENT How Jesus Met Me in My Mess	MY MESSAGE How I Can Use My Story to Comfort Others
One-sentence summary:	One-sentence summary:	One-sentence summary:

Sharing your story might seem scary at first, but you don't have to memorize a script or say everything perfectly. Simply be yourself and use your one-sentence summaries to help you remember your story. Then trust that God will use you, just as you are, to comfort someone who needs to hear the story that only you can tell.

When you choose to say yes to God—and allow your mess to become a message of comfort and hope—God takes the very things that Satan meant for evil in your life and uses them for His good and His glory. This is how God changes the world, one life at a time. And it all begins when you say yes.

THE FIVE QUESTIONS
Normal vs. Different

GROUP STUDY

GROUP DISCUSSION: *Sharing the Journey* (5 Minutes)

Welcome to Session 2 of the *What Happens When Women Say Yes to God DVD*. Sharing the journey with others is a key part of spiritual growth and discovery. Before watching the DVD, take some time to talk about your experiences since the last session. For example:

- What insights did you discover in your personal study or reading?
- What challenges or victories did you experience in applying what you learned in the last session?
- What questions would you like to ask the other members of your group?

DVD: *The Five Questions* (31 Minutes)

As you watch the DVD, use the notes on pages 24 and 25 to follow along or to add your own notes about anything that stands out to you.

NOTES

God's goal isn't to make us normal. It's to make us different so that we can make a difference.

God calls us to represent Christ everywhere we go.

Lysa has a divine appointment and shares her story with a man on a plane.

God is active in our everyday life. He arranges divine opportunities for us, and He's looking for us to say yes.

We must say, "God, I am willing. I will say yes to You."

Lysa prays this prayer every day: "God I want to <u>see You</u> today. I want to <u>hear You</u> today. I want to <u>know when You're speaking</u> to me today. God, I want to <u>know You</u>. <u>Prepare my heart to say yes to You</u>."

The internal dilemma: How do I know if it's really God speaking to me?

Five questions to help you know if God is speaking:

1. Does what I'm hearing line up with Scripture? (Romans 12:2)

   Do not conform to the pattern of this world,
      but be transformed by the renewing of your mind.
   Then you will be able to test and approve what God's will is—
   his good, pleasing and perfect will.

2. Is what I'm hearing consistent with God's character? (Galatians 5:22-23)

The fruit of the spirit is love, joy, peace, patience, kindness, goodness, faithfulness and self-control.

3. Is what I'm hearing being confirmed through other messages? (Isaiah 30:21-22)

Whether you turn to the right or to the left, your ears will hear a voice behind you saying "This is the way, walk in it."

4. Is what I'm hearing beyond me? (1 Thessalonians 5:24)

The one who calls you is faithful and he will do it.

5. Would what I'm hearing please God? (Philippians 1:9-10)

This is my prayer that your love abound more in knowledge & insight so that you may be able to discern what is best & may be pure & blameless and filled w/ the fruit of righteousness.

THIS WEEK'S ASSIGNMENT

Look for God's divine appointment to make a connection with another person. Share your story and give that person something precious to you—time, money, or a treasured possession.

GROUP DISCUSSION: *The Five Questions* (5 Minutes)

Take a few minutes to talk about what you just watched.

1. What part of the teaching had the most impact on you?

2. How do you respond to the idea that God arranges divine opportunities for us each day?

PARTNER ACTIVITY: *The Five Questions* (10 Minutes)

1. Pair up with one other person.

2. For each of the five questions listed on pages 26 and 27, take turns reading the corresponding Scripture passages. After each passage, briefly discuss what the passage teaches about how you can recognize God's voice. Note your responses in the space provided.

- Does what I'm hearing line up with Scripture? (Romans 12:2; Psalm 40:8)

- Is what I'm hearing consistent with God's character? (Galatians 5:22-23; Hebrews 13:8)

- Is what I'm hearing being confirmed through other messages I'm hearing? For example, at church, in conversations with friends, or studying in my quiet times? (Isaiah 30:21; Proverbs 15:22)

- Is what I'm hearing beyond me? (1 Thessalonians 5:24; Matthew 19:26)

- Would what I'm hearing please God? (Philippians 1:9-10; 1 Corinthians 10:31)

GROUP DISCUSSION: *The Five Questions* (7 Minutes)

1. Which of the five questions do you think will be most helpful to you in discerning whether or not a prompting is from God? How do the corresponding Bible verses help you better understand that question?

2. If you feel comfortable, share a recent experience in which you wondered if a prompting was from God. Looking back at it through the five-question filter, would you say that it was or was not from God?

3. Have you ever responded to a prompting you felt certain was from God (such as Lysa's prompting to give away her Bible)? What happened? How did it impact you and your relationship with God?

INDIVIDUAL ACTIVITY: *What I Want to Remember* (2 Minutes)

Complete this activity on your own.

1. Briefly review any notes you took.

2. In the space below, write down the most significant thing you gained in this session—from the teaching, activities, or discussions.

    What I want to remember from this session…

CLOSING PRAYER

Close your time together with prayer.

PERSONAL STUDY

READ AND REFLECT

Read chapter 2 of *What Happens When Women Say Yes to God*. If you want to dig a little deeper, use a notepad or journal to work through the Bible study at the end of the chapter. Use the space below to note any insights or questions you want to bring to the next group session.

LEARNING TO RECOGNIZE AND RESPOND TO GOD'S VOICE

Every day we have an opportunity to move beyond the normal ruts and routines of life, and we can be on the alert for divine adventure as we listen for God's voice and say yes to His invitations. When we recognize God's promptings and act on them, we no longer have to settle for a normal life. We get to be different—and make a difference—in the lives of the people God leads us to.

> God is active in our everyday lives…He delights in arranging divine opportunities to intersect with us, to interrupt us, to redirect us every day. And He's just looking for us to say yes.
>
> *What Happens When Women Say Yes to God DVD*

1. In the course of an ordinary day, how would you describe your ability to recognize the signs of God's activity or leading in your life? Circle the number below that best describes your response.

1	2	3	4	5	6	7	8	9	10

I almost never recognize God's activity and leading in my life.

Some days I recognize God's activity and leading in my life and some days I don't.

I recognize God's activity and leading in my life every day.

2. Whatever number you circled, God is eager to lead and guide you. The psalmist writes, "That is what God is like. He is our God forever and ever, and he will guide us until we die" (Psalm 48:14).

   • When you think about saying yes to God—responding to His guidance and the divine opportunities He places in your path—what thoughts or feelings come to mind?

   • How do you imagine your life and your relationship with God might change if you could routinely recognize and respond to His promptings?

3. Identify a recent prompting you received but have not yet responded to. If you can't think of one, use a past prompting but treat it as if you hadn't yet responded to it. Use the five key questions Lysa presented on the DVD to help you discern if the prompting is something God may be asking you to do. Check yes or no in response to each question. Then use the space provided to explore the reasons for your response.

YES	NO	QUESTION
❏	❏	Does what I'm hearing line up with Scripture? (Romans 12:2; Psalm 40:8)
❏	❏	Is it consistent with God's character? (Galatians 5:22-23; Hebrews 13:8)
❏	❏	Is it being confirmed through other messages I'm hearing? For example, at church, in conversations with friends, studying in my quiet times? (Isaiah 30:21; Proverbs 15:22)

YES	NO	QUESTION
❑	❑	Is it beyond me? (1 Thessalonians 5:24; Matthew 19:26)
❑	❑	Would it please God? (Philippians 1:9-10; 1 Corinthians 10:31)

Based on your use of the five questions, do you feel this prompting comes from God or from your own thoughts? In either case, what do you feel God may be asking you to do in response?

4. Learning to recognize God's voice is something we can practice and become better at. If we find it difficult at first to notice or respond to God's promptings in the moment, we can still learn something even from our missed opportunities to say yes to God. One way to do this is by practicing a review of the day with God. It is a way of praying that helps us to get better at recognizing His activity in our lives.

-   *Find a quiet place.* Choose a quiet comfortable place where you won't be interrupted or distracted.
-   *Invite God to guide you.* As you begin to review your day in God's presence, ask Him to guide and teach you. You may want to pray: *God, I want to see You. God, I want to hear You. God, I want to know You. Teach me how to see You and hear You so I can know You better and follow where You lead me.*
-   *Begin with gratitude.* Look back on your day—morning, afternoon, and evening—and notice all the ways in which you experienced God's goodness. Use the space below to express your thanks to Him for His gifts and blessings.

-   *Look for leadings.* Now go through your day again—morning, afternoon, and evening. You may want to imagine that Jesus is sitting with you while you watch a video replay of your day. When something you see catches your attention, push the "pause" button. Then ask Jesus for His guidance and insight. For example:
    -   Lord, was this a prompting from You?
    -   Is this how You wanted me to respond in this situation or to this person?
    -   Is there anything You want me to do differently next time?

Allow yourself a few moments to listen for the Lord's response. Then use the space below to note any insights or guidance you receive or to ask any additional questions that come to mind.

If you become aware of sins or failures as you review your day, humbly confess these and ask the Lord to forgive you before continuing.

- *End with praise.* Thank the Lord for being a God who reveals Himself to you, guides you, and gives you opportunities every day to say yes to Him.

When it comes to recognizing God's voice, practice doesn't make perfect, but it can make you stronger. Routinely using the five key questions to identify God's leading develops your discernment muscles. A regular practice of reviewing your day with God strengthens your ability to recognize His voice and His leading. Over time, it becomes easier to see and respond to God's promptings in the moment. And because God is always at work in your life, every activity, every conversation, and every moment provides an opportunity to say yes to God. Then, all that's left to do is to lift up your heart to the Lord and say, "God, I am willing. I will say yes to You." And the adventure begins.

LEARNING TO LIVE OPENHANDED
Good vs. God-Focused

GROUP STUDY

GROUP DISCUSSION: *Sharing the Journey* (5 Minutes)

Welcome to Session 3 of the *What Happens When Women Say Yes to God DVD*. Sharing the journey with others is a key part of spiritual growth and discovery. Before watching the DVD, take some time to talk about your experiences since the last session. For example:

- What insights did you discover in your personal study or reading?
- What challenges or victories did you experience in applying what you learned in the last session?
- What questions would you like to ask the other members of your group?

DVD: *Learning to Live Openhanded* (31 Minutes)

As you watch the DVD, use the notes on pages 36 and 37 to follow along or to add your own notes about anything that stands out to you.

NOTES

God's goal for us isn't to make us good. It's to make us God-focused.

Being good means we know the right things to do. Being God-focused means we live those right things out in our everyday lives.

God wants us to be focused on His assignments for us, looking for ways to say yes to Him at every turn.

God's assignment for Lysa: Give up TV and sell her house.

When we live life openhandedly, God rains down blessings. When we hold tightly to the things of this world, we can't catch His blessings.

The apostle Peter challenges us not to be complacent—to settle for good—but to live a God-focused life. (2 Peter 1:3-8)

Satan wants to keep us in a good, safe, comfortable place so that we never ask the question, "How can I become more God-focused?"

Awon: the Hebrew word for "sin." It means twisted, perverted, or bent down. That's how Satan wants us to be.

The more God-focused we become, the less important the things of this world are.

"Once I released something one time, I was ready to just release everything. It becomes a great adventure of saying yes!"

Lysa's daughter Hope and the $10 bill.

God says, "If you'll just be faithful with a little bit, I'll trust you with so much more." (Matthew 25:21; Luke 16:10)

THIS WEEK'S ASSIGNMENT

Say to God, "Here is something I know I'm supposed to release." Then release it. Practice living openhandedly.

GROUP DISCUSSION: *Learning to Live Openhanded* (5 Minutes)

Take a few minutes to talk about what you just watched.

1. What part of the teaching had the most impact on you?

2. How did you respond to Lysa's story of giving up television and putting her house up for sale?

INDIVIDUAL ACTIVITY: *Faith Continuums* (3 Minutes)

Complete this activity on your own.

1. Listed below are words that contrast a faith that is merely good with a faith that is God-focused. Place a mark on each continuum to indicate where you think you're at.

GOOD		GOD-FOCUSED
Not making waves	o————————————o	Making a difference
Following the rules	o————————————o	Following God's promptings
Religion	o————————————o	Relationship
Head knowledge	o————————————o	Heart knowledge
Think about it	o————————————o	Live it out
Self-protection	o————————————o	Self-sacrifice
Duty	o————————————o	Delight
Routine	o————————————o	Adventure
Closed-fisted	o————————————o	Openhanded
Complacent	o————————————o	Looking for ways to say yes

2. Circle the continuum on page 38 that stands out most to you for any reason. In the space below, briefly note what it is that catches your attention.

Group Discussion: *Faith Continuums* (6 Minutes)

1. What would you say is the appeal of faith that is merely good? In other words, why do you think we might settle for being good rather than God-focused?

2. Which descriptions of God-focused faith appeal most to you? Why?

3. If you feel comfortable, share any observations from your responses on the continuums. What stands out most to you? Why?

Group Discussion: *Releasing Lesser Things* (8 Minutes)

1. On the DVD, Lysa tells the story of how her daughter Hope refused to let go of the $10 bill she received for her birthday, which ultimately caused her to miss out on a $50 bill waiting for her at home. Have there been times in your walk of faith when you behaved like Hope—refusing to release something of lesser importance and perhaps missing out on a greater blessing? What happened?

2. The more enamored we are of God, the easier it is to let go of the stuff of this world. The apostle Paul echoes this theme in his letter to the Philippians. Read the passage below aloud:

> Yes, everything else is worthless when compared with the infinite value of knowing Christ Jesus my Lord. For his sake I have discarded everything else, counting it all as garbage, so that I could gain Christ and become one with him. I no longer count on my own righteousness through obeying the law; rather, I become righteous through faith in Christ. For God's way of making us right with himself depends on faith (Philippians 3:8-9).

To get a fresh perspective on this familiar passage, read it aloud again, this time from *The Message*:

> Yes, all the things I once thought were so important are gone from my life. Compared to the high privilege of knowing Christ Jesus as my Master, first-hand, everything I once thought I had going for me is insignificant—dog dung. I've dumped it all in the trash so that I could embrace Christ and be embraced by him. I didn't want some petty, inferior brand of righteousness that comes from keeping a list of rules when I could get the robust kind that comes from trusting Christ—God's righteousness (Philippians 3:8-9 MSG).

3. How does this passage impact your understanding of what it means to be God-focused?

4. What kinds of things do you think you may be focused on, attached to, or relying on besides Christ? How might releasing these things—holding them with open hands—enable you to receive the greater blessing of a more intimate relationship with Christ?

INDIVIDUAL ACTIVITY: *What I Want to Remember* (2 Minutes)

Complete this activity on your own.

1. Briefly review any notes you took.

2. In the space below, write down the most significant thing you gained in this session—from the teaching, activities, or discussions.

> What I want to remember from this session…

CLOSING PRAYER

Close your time together with prayer.

PERSONAL STUDY

READ AND REFLECT

Read chapters 3 and 8 of *What Happens When Women Say Yes to God*. If you want to dig a little deeper, use a notepad or journal to work through the Bible studies at the end of the chapters. Use the space below to note any insights or questions you want to bring to the next group session.

LEARNING TO LIVE OPENHANDEDLY

Saying yes to God is an act of love and worship. When we surrender to Him, we acknowledge that He knows what's best for us and that everything we have belongs to Him. Our posture is openhanded, enabling us to receive God's many blessings—blessings that enable us to know and experience Him every day.

> God wants to know if we're willing to give
> up what we love to Him who loves us more.
> He desires for us to open our fists and
> trust Him with absolutely everything.
>
> *What Happens When Women Say Yes to God,* page 49

1. Lysa prayed, "God, how can I be more God-focused? What do You require of me?" She then felt God asking her to do two things: give up TV and put her house up for sale.

   Using the list below as a prompt, take a few moments to think through the various aspects of your life. Can you identify something you would consider releasing—something you love or enjoy that you could give up to Him who loves you more? Try to identify three to five things for each category. For now, think of this as brainstorming. You're not committing to anything. You're just identifying a list of ideas you can consider later.

   Daily or weekly habits and routines I might release...

   Examples: Buying a cup of coffee or eating out, watching certain TV shows, consuming soft drinks, etc.

   Possessions I might release...

   Examples: Clothing, money, jewelry, investments, appliances or electronics, a vehicle, a home, etc.

   Activities I might release...

   Examples: Shopping (for entertainment rather than for necessities), idly chatting on the phone, web-surfing, etc.

Other things I might release…

What thoughts or emotions come to mind when you think about the possibility of releasing some of these things?

We need not fear what our obedience will cause
to happen in our lives. We should only fear what
our disobedience will cause us to miss.

What Happens When Women Say Yes to God, page 45

---

2. The Bible tells the story of a God-focused woman who gave up something precious to her in a beautiful act of worship and surrender:

> A dinner was prepared in Jesus' honor. Martha served, and Lazarus was among those who ate with him. Then Mary took a twelve-ounce jar of expensive perfume made from essence of nard, and she anointed Jesus' feet with it, wiping his feet with her hair. The house was filled with the fragrance (John 12:2-3).

> The perfume was exceedingly precious. It was made from a plant grown in India called nard or spikenard* and it was worth a year's wages (John 12:5). We know from another account

---

* "A costly perennial herb with an aromatic root, native to East India and presently cultivated on the Himalayas…The ointment is stored in an alabaster jar to preserve its fragrance. Mary's anointing of Jesus with the precious nard was an act of real sacrifice." *The New International Dictionary of the Bible,* "Spikenard" (Grand Rapids: Zondervan, 1987), 804.

of this story that the perfume was contained in an alabaster jar (Mark 14:3). Alabaster is a soft mineral, easily carved and commonly used in Jesus' day to create containers for precious ointments.* The jar Mary used would have been shaped like a flask with a long, thin neck. It was sealed and contained enough nard for just one use. In order to use the perfume, it was necessary for Mary to break the neck of the flask.†

This is not merely a treasured possession for Mary. It likely represents her life savings and may have been her only security. Her devotion is both sacrificial and risky as she literally pours her future onto Jesus' feet and then is harshly rebuked by others for her extravagance (Mark 14:5). Jesus, however, defends and praises her:

> "Leave her alone," said Jesus. "Why are you bothering her? She has done a beautiful thing to me…I tell you the truth, wherever the gospel is preached throughout the world, what she has done will also be told, in memory of her" (Mark 14:6,9 NIV).

- If you could imagine this story taking place in our day, what kind of things do you think a contemporary Mary might lay at Jesus' feet?

- Once broken, the flask could not be reused or resealed. Mary could not change her mind or salvage a portion of the contents. In breaking the neck of the flask, she severed her attachment to something that was exceedingly precious to her and became free to attach herself more deeply, intimately, and authentically to Jesus.

---

* *The New International Dictionary of the Bible*, "Alabaster," 657.
† Kenneth Barker, gen. ed., *The NIV Study Bible*, footnote for Mark 14:3 (Grand Rapids: Zondervan, 1995), 1519.

Can you imagine yourself in Mary's place? What might you have been thinking and feeling as you broke the flask?

What would it be like to feel so deeply connected to Jesus?

• Mary's act of sacrifice and worship is devoted to Christ, but it benefits everyone around her as the fragrance fills the entire house. How does this aspect of the story help you to understand how God uses our sacrifices to not only to draw us closer to Him but to also help others?

God doesn't want us to just be good people.
He wants us to be so God-focused that we say,
"Jesus, whatever it is, whatever it costs me,
I trust You enough to know I can say yes."

What Happens When Women Say Yes to God DVD

3. Take a moment to briefly review your responses to question 1 (pages 42-43). For each category of things you wrote down, identify one or two things you are willing to consider releasing in order to become more God-focused. Write those things in the first column. In the second column, imagine how this sacrifice might help you to become more deeply connected to Jesus. You're not making any decisions or commitments yet, you're just narrowing down the potential options.

What I Want to Consider Releasing	How I Think Releasing This Might Free Me to Become More Attached to Jesus
Daily or weekly habits and routines I might release...	
Possessions I might release...	
Activities I might release...	
Other things I might release...	

- As you review your responses on the chart, what emotions are you aware of? For example, do you feel fear, excitement, dread, anticipation, or something else?

- Briefly set aside your study materials. Take a moment to be quiet and to listen for God's leading. Tell Him about the items you wrote down and any emotions you're aware of. You may want to symbolically hold your hands open before you as you ask for God's guidance. You might pray a prayer like this:

  God, I want to be focused on You. You know everything I've written on my chart—and everything I haven't written. Please guide me and help me to know what You require of me. I want so much to be free so I can be deeply connected to You.

  After a time of quiet listening, use the space below to note any impressions or next steps you feel God may be asking you to take.

God wants so much more for you than just the good life. He wants you to be free—completely free of anything that might hold you back from the great things He has for you. He doesn't want you to miss one single blessing of a God-focused life. Most of all, He wants you to trust Him with that risky, passionate devotion that Mary had—the kind of love and trust that says, "Lord, my past, my future, and everything I have are Yours. Let the adventure begin."

SIMPLE ACTS OF OBEDIENCE CHANGE THE WORLD
Happy vs. Holy

GROUP STUDY

GROUP DISCUSSION: *Sharing the Journey* (5 Minutes)

Welcome to Session 4 of the *What Happens When Women Say Yes to God DVD*. Sharing the journey with others is a key part of spiritual growth and discovery. Before watching the DVD, take some time to talk about your experiences since the last session. For example:

- What insights did you discover in your personal study or reading?
- What challenges or victories did you experience in applying what you learned in the last session?
- What questions would you like to ask the other members of your group?

DVD: *Simple Acts of Obedience Change the World* (31 Minutes)

As you watch the DVD, use the notes on the next page to follow along or to add your own notes about anything that stands out to you.

NOTES

God's goal isn't to make us happy. He wants to make us holy.

God often uses things that don't necessarily feel good, comfortable, or easy to make us holy.

Holy: to be set apart for a noble use or a noble purpose.

Story of going to the Liberian Boys' Choir concert.

Sometimes saying yes to God is really hard. It's really inconvenient. It can make no sense.

"But God..." When you put those two words together, things that don't make sense suddenly make sense.

"Blessed are the pure in heart, for they will see God" (Matthew 5:8 NIV).

When a woman says yes to God, she doesn't have to worry about changing the world because God is going to do it.

THIS WEEK'S ASSIGNMENT

Open up your home in some way.

Group Discussion: *Simple Acts of Obedience Change the World* (5 Minutes)

Take a few minutes to talk about what you just watched.

1. What part of the teaching had the most impact on you?

2. How do you respond to the idea that God often uses things that don't feel good or comfortable to make us holy?

Individual Activity: *Blessed Are the Pure in Heart* (4 Minutes)

Complete this activity on your own.

1. God's goal is to make us holy—set apart for a noble use. Holiness does not mean we have to be perfect people, but holiness does require something of us. Here's how the apostle Paul describes it:

> Let us purify ourselves from everything that contaminates body and spirit, perfecting holiness out of reverence for God (2 Corinthians 7:1 NIV).

The purity required for holiness begins with the heart. Listed below are four translations of Matthew 5:8. As you read each one, underline any words or phrases that stand out to you.

> God blesses those whose hearts are pure, for they will see God (NLT).
>
> Blessed (happy, enviably fortunate, and spiritually prosperous—possessing the happiness produced by the experience of God's favor and especially conditioned by the revelation of His grace, regardless of their outward conditions) are the pure in heart, for they shall see God! (AMP).
>
> You're blessed when you get your inside world—your mind and heart—put right. Then you can see God in the outside world (MSG).
>
> Happy the clean in heart—because they shall see God (Young's).

2. Based on what you read, how would you complete the sentence below and on page 52?

   If I were blessed, I would be/feel/experience…

If I were pure in heart, I would be/feel/experience...

GROUP DISCUSSION: *Blessed Are the Pure in Heart* (5 Minutes)

1. Read aloud the four translations of Matthew 5:8 listed on page 51.

2. According to this verse, what do you think it means to be blessed? How might a woman recognize this kind of blessedness in her own life?

3. What do you think it means to be pure in heart? If you know someone who exemplifies this, describe what you see that leads you to characterize him or her as pure in heart.

GROUP DISCUSSION: *Choosing Holiness* (8 Minutes)

1. In her teaching, Lysa describes how she faced a moment of decision. Read the following quote aloud:

   > After the concert, I remember taking my little girls' hands and walking out into the aisle of the church. I looked toward the back door, and I knew I could so easily walk back into my easy, safe, comfortable life. But then I looked toward the front of that church, and I thought, *This is what a woman who says yes to God does, because God doesn't want to make me just good. He wants to make me holy. Set apart for a noble and good use.*

2. Recall a recent or past experience in which you faced a similar choice between happiness (your easy, safe, comfortable life) and holiness (allowing God to use you for a noble purpose). How did you know it was a happiness-versus-holiness kind of choice? What thoughts went through your mind as you wrestled with your decision?

3. When you imagine the kind of happiness-versus-holiness choices that might come your way in the future, what fears or concerns come to mind? What excites you about the divine adventure these choices might bring into your life?

INDIVIDUAL ACTIVITY: *What I Want to Remember* (2 Minutes)

Complete this activity on your own.

1. Briefly review any notes you took.

2. In the space below, write down the most significant thing you gained in this session—from the teaching, activities, or discussions.

   What I want to remember from this session…

CLOSING PRAYER

Close your time together with prayer.

PERSONAL STUDY

READ AND REFLECT

Read chapter 4 of *What Happens When Women Say Yes to God*. If you want to dig a little deeper, use a notepad or journal to work through the Bible study at the end of the chapter. Use the space below to note any insights or questions you want to bring to the next group session.

SAYING YES TO HOLINESS

Saying yes to God is always the right thing to do, but it's not always the easiest thing to do. In fact, sometimes it's really hard, uncomfortable, or inconvenient. But God has a purpose in those difficult moments. He uses them to challenge us, refine our hearts, and make us holy—pure-in-heart women He can use for a noble purpose.

There is no end to what God can
do with you—if you let Him.

What Happens When Women Say Yes to God, page 59

---

1. Do you believe the statement above is true and not just for God's people in general but for you specifically? Check the box below that best describes the degree to which you believe this statement is true for you.

   ❏ I disagree strongly.

   ❏ I disagree somewhat.

   ❏ I neither agree nor disagree.

   ❏ I agree somewhat.

   ❏ I agree strongly.

Briefly describe the reason for your response.

I imagine God scanning the whole earth…
and saying, "I don't need the person who has
a perfect background and perfect qualifications
and everything all arranged and organized. I
don't need [only] the woman who has her spices
alphabetized and never gets them out of order.
I just need a woman who will say yes. That's
the woman I can use to change the world."

What Happens When Women Say Yes to God DVD

---

2. At the time Lysa and Art considered adopting two boys from Liberia, Lysa already felt over-whelmed with parenting her three girls. Even her friends questioned whether she had what

it took to be a mom of two teenage boys. Still, Lysa said yes to God, even though what He wanted her to do wasn't something for which she felt completely qualified. How do you feel about the idea that God might ask you to step out of your comfort zone to say yes to Him?

God's goal isn't necessarily to make us happy but rather to make us holy, positioning us to be set apart to be used for a high and noble reason.

What Happens When Women Say Yes to God DVD

---

3. One of the qualifications God requires of us is holiness. Read the verses below slowly and prayerfully. You may want to say them aloud or read them over more than once. Underline any words or phrases that stand out to you.

> Now you must be holy in everything you do, just as God who chose you is holy. For the Scriptures say, "You must be holy because I am holy" (1 Peter 1:15-16).

> Who may climb the mountain of the LORD? Who may stand in his holy place? Only those whose hands and hearts are pure, who do not worship idols and never tell lies. They will receive the LORD's blessing and have a right relationship with God their savior (Psalm 24:3-5).

> Teach me your ways, O LORD, that I may live according to your truth! Grant me purity of heart, so that I may honor you (Psalm 86:11).

> Come close to God, and God will come close to you. Wash your hands, you sinners; purify your hearts, for your loyalty is divided between God and the world (James 4:8).

> Rejoice in the LORD and be glad, all you who obey him! Shout for joy, all you whose hearts are pure! (Psalm 32:11).

- Drawing on the verses above, list three to five words or phrases under each sentence below to describe what holiness is and is not.

      Holiness is...   **Holiness is not...**

- What connections do these verses make between holiness of heart and holiness of behavior?

- What might be God's invitation to you through these verses? What would it mean to say yes to that invitation?

> A lot of times in life, things happen to interrupt
> us, to challenge us, to step on our toes a little bit.
> And what might be good for us doesn't always
> feel good at the time. But it's often the things
> that don't necessarily feel good, comfortable, or
> easy at the time that God uses to make us holy.
>
> *What Happens When Women Say Yes to God DVD*

4. The assignment for this session is to say yes to God by opening your home in some small way. This may happen on the spur of the moment as God leads someone across your path, or in a more intentional way as you ask God to guide you in identifying potential opportunities ahead of time.

Take a moment to think about the places you routinely come in contact with people. For example, your neighborhood, church, school, work, the fitness center, grocery store, or restaurant. Review the example below and then use the chart on the next page to begin thinking about who you might reach out to and how you might use your home as a way to say yes to God this week.

EXAMPLE

PLACES	PEOPLE	IDEAS FOR HOW I MIGHT OPEN MY HOME
My neighborhood	*Sandy, the single mom with two kids who lives down the street*	*Invite Sandy and the kids to dinner on a weeknight so she doesn't have to cook, or offer to watch the kids one evening so she can have some time to herself.*

PLACES	PEOPLE	IDEAS FOR HOW I MIGHT OPEN MY HOME

- Briefly review what you wrote on the chart. Circle the two or three places or people you want to focus on.
- Pray about the places or people you circled. Ask God to lead you into opportunities to use your home for Him this week.

Saying yes to God means saying yes to holiness—and all the challenges that sometimes come our way as a result. We may not always be happy about the hardships tied up in those challenges, but they are God's way of purifying us, drawing us closer to Him, and transforming us into women He can use for a noble purpose every day. And that's about more than mere happiness—it's 100 percent pure joy.

I WANT TO SAY YES, BUT I'M AFRAID

Self-Confident vs. God-Confident

GROUP STUDY

GROUP DISCUSSION: *Sharing the Journey* (5 Minutes)

Welcome to Session 5 of the *What Happens When Women Say Yes to God DVD*. Sharing the journey with others is a key part of spiritual growth and discovery. Before watching the DVD, take some time to talk about your experiences since the last session. For example:

- What insights did you discover in your personal study or reading?
- What challenges or victories did you experience in applying what you learned in the last session?
- What questions would you like to ask the other members of your group?

DVD: *I Want to Say Yes, but I'm Afraid* (29 Minutes)

As you watch the DVD, use the notes on pages 62-64 to follow along or to add your own notes about anything that stands out to you.

Notes

The one thing that holds us back from saying yes to God more than anything else: fear.

Key passage: "God has not given us a spirit of fear, but of power and of love and of a sound mind" (2 Timothy 1:7 NKJV).

God's goal isn't to make us self-confident. It's to make us God-confident.

"Who is going to harm you if you are eager to do good? But even if you should suffer for what is right, you are blessed. 'Do not fear what they fear; do not be frightened.' But in your hearts set apart Christ as Lord. Always be prepared to give an answer to everyone who asks you to give the reason for the hope that you have" (1 Peter 3:13-15 NIV).

We don't have to walk in self-confidence. We can walk in God-confidence because God has given us power, love, and a sound mind.

- Power

   When we are thankful, we acknowledge that God holds all the power. (Philippians 4:5-6)

   The Lord is near.

Our job is obedience. God's job is results.

- Love

If we really knew how much God loves us, we would be the most unafraid people.

We aren't just women who have been thrown into this world. We are women with a high calling, with a holy purpose, with a divine Father who loves us and wants us to rest in that love.

- Sound Mind

Jesus came so that we would have truth. (John 18:37)

The more we fill our minds with truth, the less room we will have for fear to redirect us and make us women who say no to God.

Story of the seed in the seed packet.

What happens when women say yes to God? They stop relying on themselves. They keep their fear in perspective.

This Week's Assignment

Identify an assignment from sessions 1 through 4 that you didn't do because of fear. Push past your fear and do that assignment. If you already completed all the assignments, pick one assignment and take it up a notch. Intentionally place yourself in a position to have to walk in God-confidence.

Group Discussion: *I Want to Say Yes, but I'm Afraid* (5 Minutes)

Take a few minutes to talk about what you just watched.

1. What part of the teaching had the most impact on you?

2. How do you respond to the idea that we can be God-confident rather than self-confident?

Partner Activity: *The Three Components of God-Confidence* (11 Minutes)

1. Pair up with one other person.

2. The key to facing our fears and living with God-confidence is to remember what God has given us: "God has not given us a spirit of fear, but of *power* and of *love* and of *a sound mind*" (2 Timothy 1:7 NKJV, emphasis added).

   For the three items on pages 64-66—power, love, and sound mind—take turns reading the corresponding Scripture passages aloud. Then briefly discuss the questions that follow. Note your responses in the space provided.

   ### Power

   > Don't worry or be afraid of their threats. Instead, you must worship Christ as Lord of your life (1 Peter 3:14-15).

   > Don't worry about anything; instead, pray about everything. Tell God what you need, and thank him for all he has done. Then you will experience God's peace, which exceeds anything we can understand. His peace will guard your hearts and minds as you live in Christ Jesus (Philippians 4:6-7).

God is awesome in his sanctuary. The God of Israel gives power and strength to his people. Praise be to God! (Psalm 68:35).

Based on these verses, how would you describe the connection between fear, worship (or thanksgiving), and power?

LOVE

I am convinced that nothing can ever separate us from God's love. Neither death nor life, neither angels nor demons, neither our fears for today nor our worries about tomorrow—not even the powers of hell can separate us from God's love. No power in the sky above or in the earth below—indeed, nothing in all creation will ever be able to separate us from the love of God that is revealed in Christ Jesus our Lord (Romans 8:38-39).

He takes no pleasure in the strength of a horse or in human might. No, the Lord's delight is in those who fear him, those who put their hope in his unfailing love (Psalm 147:10-11).

Based on these verses, how would you describe the connection between fear and God's love?

SOUND MIND

> "You are a king, then!" said Pilate. Jesus answered, "You say that I am a king. In fact, the reason I was born, and for this I came into the world, to testify to the truth. Everyone on the side of truth listens to me" (John 18:37 NIV).

> Show me the right path, O LORD; point out the road for me to follow. Lead me by your truth and teach me, for you are the God who saves me. All day long I put my hope in you (Psalm 25:4-5).

Based on these verses, how would you describe the connection between fear and a sound mind rooted in God's truth?

GROUP DISCUSSION: *The Three Components of God-Confidence* (8 Minutes)

1. Which of the three components of God-confidence—power, love, or a sound mind—do you need most? Why?

2. How might this component help you overcome your fears of saying yes to God?

3. Did fear prevent you from completing any of the assignments from the previous four sessions (telling your story, giving away something precious to you, releasing something, opening your home)? If so, how might you overcome your fear this week by leaning into God-confidence? If not, how did God-confidence help you overcome your fears?

INDIVIDUAL ACTIVITY: *What I Want to Remember* (2 Minutes)

Complete this activity on your own.

1. Briefly review any notes you took.
2. In the space below, write down the most significant thing you gained in this session—from the teaching, activities, or discussions.

> What I want to remember from this session…

CLOSING PRAYER

Close your time together with prayer.

PERSONAL STUDY

READ AND REFLECT

Read chapters 5 and 6 of *What Happens When Women Say Yes to God*. If you want to dig a little deeper, use a notepad or journal to work through the Bible studies at the end of the chapters. Use the space below to note any insights or questions you want to bring to the next group session.

SHIFTING FOCUS

Fear and faith are both a matter of focus—specifically, where we choose to place our focus. Overcoming our fears so we can say yes to God means shifting our focus from ourselves and what we're afraid of to God and all He's capable of.

The more we focus on the object of our fear, the bigger and more magnified that fear becomes. But when we shift from focusing on our fear to focusing on God, the bigger and more magnified God becomes. This puts our fear in perspective.

What Happens When Women Say Yes to God DVD

---

1. Generally speaking, how would you describe the role that fear has played in your life? Check the box next to the statement below that best describes your response.

   ❏ Fear is almost always an issue in my life. I find it very difficult or impossible to overcome my fears.

   ❏ Fear is frequently an issue in my life. Overcoming my fears is hard to do.

   ❏ Fear is occasionally an issue in my life. I have to overcome fears from time to time.

   ❏ Fear is rarely an issue in my life. I am almost always able to overcome my fears and move on.

2. In terms of self-confidence vs. God-confidence, where would you say you are right now? Mark an X on the continuum below to indicate your response.

SELF-CONFIDENCE
When I am afraid, I
feel I have only myself
to rely on.

GOD-CONFIDENCE
When I am afraid, I am
able to overcome my
fears by relying on God.

One of the most radical blessings for the woman saying yes to God is the peace that rushes though the soul of the one who is attentive to the Lord's commands.

What Happens When Women Say Yes to God, page 84

---

3. The apostle Paul contrasts living by the flesh and living by the Spirit in a way that could also be used to describe the difference between being self-confident (focused on self) and God-confident (focused on God). Read the passage below, first in the New International Version and then in its adapted form:

   Those who live according to the sinful nature have their minds set on what that nature desires; but those who live in accordance with the Spirit have their minds set on what the Spirit desires. The mind of sinful man is death, but the mind controlled by the Spirit is life and peace (Romans 8:5-6 NIV).

Those who live according to *self-confidence* have their minds set on what the *self* desires; but those who live in accordance with *God-confidence* have their minds set on what *God* desires. The mind governed by *self-confidence* is death, but the mind governed by *God-confidence* is life and peace (Romans 8:5-6, adapted).

Based on this passage, how would you describe the relationship between God-confidence and peace?

4. According to the Romans 8 passage, a mind set on the self is one devoted to things that are human rather than divine, fleeting rather than eternal. The mind that is self-focused can't be God-focused. Here is how *The Message* describes this dynamic:

Those who trust God's action in them find that God's Spirit is in them—living and breathing God! Obsession with self in these matters is a dead end; attention to God leads us out into the open, into a spacious, free life. Focusing on the self is the opposite of focusing on God. Anyone completely absorbed in self ignores God, ends up thinking more about self than God (Romans 8:5-7 MSG).

When fear keeps us from saying yes to God, it could be a sign that we are focused on ourselves—our worries, fears, and limitations—rather than God. Use the chart on page 71 to explore how fear might be impacting your ability to focus on God and to identify how your life would be different if you could overcome your fears with God's help.

AREA OF LIFE	MY FEARS How "Self-Confidence" Keeps Me Focused on Myself What particular fears are you aware of in this area of life?	MY PEACE How God-Confidence Can Help Me Focus on God What would be different in your life if you could overcome this fear with God's help?
Relationships (family, friends, colleagues)		
Finances		
Work or daily life		
Health		
Relationship with God		
Ministry/faith in action		
My future		
My past		
Other		

When we face a fear, it's not bad to feel afraid. That's natural. But we don't have to stay focused on that fear. Instead, we can redirect our focus to a mighty God who loves us. A God who whispers straight to our hearts, "Don't be afraid, for I am with you. Don't be discouraged, for I am your God. I will strengthen you and help you. I will hold you up with my victorious right hand" (Isaiah 41:10).

WHAT DOES GOD WANT *ME* TO DO?

God Wants Us to Say Yes

GROUP STUDY

GROUP DISCUSSION: *Sharing the Journey* (5 Minutes)

Welcome to Session 6 of the *What Happens When Women Say Yes to God DVD*. Sharing the journey with others is a key part of spiritual growth and discovery. Before watching the DVD, take some time to talk about your experiences since the last session. For example:

- What insights did you discover in your personal study or reading?

- What challenges or victories did you experience in applying what you learned in the last session?

- What questions would you like to ask the other members of your group?

DVD: *What Does God Want* Me *to Do?* (33 Minutes)

As you watch the DVD, use the notes on pages 74 and 75 to follow along or to add your own notes about anything that stands out to you.

NOTES

God wants His people to live to say yes to Him.

God's will is all about how He wants us to be. What we are supposed to do will unfold from there.

"Be joyful always; pray continually; give thanks in all circumstances, for this is God's will for you in Christ Jesus" (1 Thessalonians 5:16-18 NIV).

- Story of Lysa's daughter's gymnastics injury.

- "Consider it pure joy, my brothers [and sisters], whenever you face trials of many kinds, because you know that the testing of your faith produces perseverance. Perseverance must finish its work so that you may be mature and complete, not lacking anything" (James 1:2-4 NIV).

- "'Though the mountains be shaken and the hills be removed, yet my unfailing love for you will not be shaken nor my covenant of peace removed,' says the LORD, who has compassion on you" (Isaiah 54:10 NIV).

Pray continually.

- God says, "Just be with Me." (Psalm 46:10)

- Every day, moment by moment, we can pray, "God I want to see You. I need to hear You. I need Your truth. I need to know You right now. Help me say yes and follow hard after You even in this situation."

Be thankful. Give thanks in all circumstances.

- Recognize what God has already done.

- Sometimes when we have too many blessings, we forget to be thankful.

Sometimes saying yes to God means to simply be in the center of His will in the small, every-day things.

If we want to be unusual—different, holy, and set apart for an amazing work of the Lord—we must be joyful, prayerful, and thankful every day.

Life is like making a cake.

- It takes all different kinds of ingredients to make a life—dry times, sweet times, and yucky times.

- We say to Jesus, "I am going to trust You and be a woman who says yes to God no matter what kind of time I'm going through."

This Week's Assignment

Go out and multiply this message.

Group Discussion: *What Does God Want Me to Do?* (5 Minutes)

Take a few minutes to talk about what you just watched.

1. What part of the teaching had the most impact on you?

2. How do you respond to the idea that God's will for us is as much about who He wants us to *be* as it is what He wants us to *do*?

Individual Activity: *Are You Following God's Will?* (3 Minutes)

Complete this activity on your own.

1. According to the apostle Paul, God's will for us is to "Be joyful always; pray continually; give thanks in all circumstances" (1 Thessalonians 5:16-18 NIV). The words *always*, *continually*, and *all* emphasize how comprehensive these things are meant to be in our lives. God's will is that we be at 100 percent capacity in our joy, prayer, and gratitude.

   Take a moment to do a brief assessment of your joy, prayer, and gratitude. Are you at 10 percent of capacity? Ninety percent? Somewhere in between? The example meter below shows a prayer capacity of just more than 50 percent, indicating this person prays quite a bit but could pray more. Draw arrows on the three meters below the example to indicate the degree to which you practice joy, prayer, and gratitude.

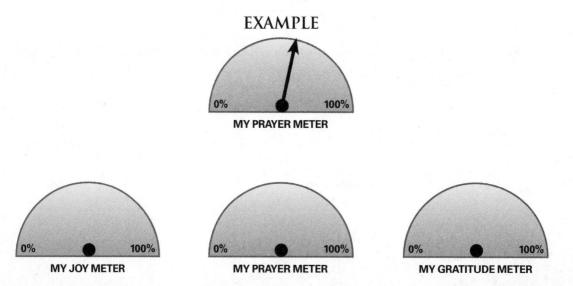

2. Based on your three meters, how would you respond to the question, "Are you following God's will?"

GROUP DISCUSSION: *Are You Following God's Will?* (12 Minutes)

1. God's will is as much about being as it is about doing. He wants us to *be* the kind of women who will *do* His will. How does this truth impact your understanding of what it means to be in the center of God's will?

2. Which of the three practices—joy, prayer, and gratitude—is easiest for you? Which is the hardest? Why?

3. If you feel comfortable, share any insights you gained from completing the three meters in the individual activity. How would you describe where you're at in terms of following God's will? In what ways do you want to move even closer to the center of God's will for you in the days ahead?

INDIVIDUAL ACTIVITY: *What I Want to Remember* (2 Minutes)

Complete this activity on your own.

1. Briefly review any notes you took.

2. In the space below, write down the most significant thing you gained in this session—from the teaching, activities, or discussions.

> What I want to remember from this session...

CLOSING PRAYER

Close your time together with prayer.

PERSONAL STUDY

READ AND REFLECT

Read chapters 7 and 9 of *What Happens When Women Say Yes to God*. If you want to dig a little deeper, use a notepad or journal to work through the Bible studies at the end of the chapters. Use the space below to note any insights or questions you want to bring to the next group session.

MOVING TO THE CENTER

Once we learn how to say yes to God and commit ourselves to living that out, we start to wonder, *What does God want me to do? What is God's will for me? Is there some big assignment God wants me to complete? How will I know?*

The good news is that God's will is not a mystery. We can move closer to the center of His will every day by becoming women steeped in joy, prayer, and gratitude.

God's will is all about how God wants us to be.
When we are the kind of person who determines
to be in the center of God's will, what we are
supposed to do will unfold from there.

What Happens When Women Say Yes to God DVD

---

1. The apostle Paul describes three key components of becoming the kind of people God wants us to become: "Be joyful always; pray continually; give thanks in all circumstances, for this is God's will for you in Christ Jesus" (1 Thessalonians 5:16-18 NIV).

   How do these three things—joy, prayer, and gratitude—build on and reinforce each other? For example, how might continuous prayer impact your experience of joy and your ability to express thanks in all circumstances?

Hard times are not the time to push the pause button on this great adventure with God…We can find joy in the midst of our circumstances. This is God's will for His people who want to live with a yes-heart.

What Happens When Women Say Yes to God DVD

---

2. It may be surprising to think of joy as something we experience not in the absence of trials but in the midst of them. But some Bible scholars believe it's actually impossible to experience true joy any other way.* In difficult times, we can experience joy by saying "a defiant Nevertheless."† *I am struggling; nevertheless, God is good to me. I am hurting; nevertheless, I know God loves me. I am confused; nevertheless, I know God is with me.*

---

* "The Pauline Epistles testify to the paradox that Christian joy is to be found only in the midst of sadness, affliction and care. Indeed, this is precisely where it gives proof of its power." Erich Beyreuther and Günther Finkenrath, "Joy," *New International Dictionary of New Testament Theology, Volume 2*, Colin Brown, gen. ed. (Grand Rapids, MI: Zondervan, 1986), 359.

† Karl Barth, *The Epistle to the Philippians* (Richmond, VA: John Knox Press, 1962), 120. Quoted in "Joy," Erich Beyreuther and Günther Finkenrath, *New International Dictionary of New Testament Theology*, Volume 2, Colin Brown, gen. ed. (Grand Rapids, MI: Zondervan, 1986), 359.

Every difficulty is an opportunity to practice joy, to say a resounding "nevertheless." What nevertheless statements could you make about your life right now?

The apostle James affirms the connection between joy and suffering:

> Consider it pure joy, my brothers [and sisters], whenever you face trials of many kinds, because you know that the testing of your faith develops perseverance. Perseverance must finish its work so that you may be mature and complete, not lacking anything (James 1:2-4 NIV).

Referring back to your "nevertheless" statements above, in what ways might these experiences be producing perseverance, maturity, and completeness in you?

Prayer isn't something [for which] we have to sit down and find all the official words and do it just right. God says, "Just be with Me."…It's an everyday conversation.

What Happens When Women Say Yes to God DVD

---

3. For now, rather than thinking or writing about prayer, take a moment to actually pray. Set aside your study materials and enjoy spending time in God's presence. You might want to begin by praying, "God, in this moment, I want to see You, hear You, know You." Then listen and respond as He leads. When you are finished, use the space below to note any observations about your time with Him.

Sometimes, when we have too many
blessings, we become so overwhelmed with
our blessings that we forget to be thankful.

What Happens When Women Say Yes to God DVD

---

4. Imagine taking time to shop for the perfect birthday gift for a friend. Which of the two responses below would you rather receive in a thank-you note:

   Thanks for the gift.

   Thanks so much for the beautiful silver earrings. I love the intricate design. They're just my style and I know I'll wear them a lot!

   The first statement expresses the bare minimum level of gratitude; in fact, it might leave you wondering if the person really did like the gift. But the second statement leaves no room for doubt—your gift was noticed and deeply appreciated.

   God accepts every expression of gratitude, but He loves to know that His gifts are noticed and appreciated just as we do. One way to do this is to "get small"—to focus on the everyday gifts and graces we sometimes take for granted. For example, a perfectly timed hug, nourishing food in the pantry, or the comforting softness of a handmade sweater. Using the prompts on page 82, take a few moments to get small with your gratitude.

Things I am grateful for within the last week...

Things I am grateful for within the last 24 hours...

Things I am grateful for within the last hour...

Things I am grateful for in this very moment...

The adventure of saying yes to God never ends. It begins again with each new day and continues as we respond to the divine invitations God weaves into every moment…

Are you willing to become comfort-able? Will you share your story to encourage someone else?

Are you willing to be different so that I can use you to make a difference?

Are you willing to be God-focused, actively looking for ways to live out your faith?

Are you willing to be pure in heart, devoted to holiness so I can use you for a noble purpose?

Are you willing to be God-confident, to keep your attention focused on Me rather than yourself?

Are you willing to move closer to the center of My will for you every day by filling your days with joy, prayer, and gratitude?

Are you willing to say yes?

ABOUT THE AUTHOR

Lysa TerKeurst is wife to Art and mom to five priority blessings named Jackson, Mark, Hope, Ashley, and Brooke. The author of 14 books, she has been featured on *Focus on the Family*, *Good Morning America*, *The Oprah Show*, and in *O* magazine. Her passion is inspiring women to say yes to God and take part in the awesome adventure God has designed every soul to live. While she is president of Proverbs 31 Ministries, to those who know her best she is simply a carpooling mom who loves her family, loves Jesus passionately, and struggles like the rest of us with laundry, junk drawers, and cellulite.

Website: If you enjoyed this resource by Lysa, you'll love all the additional resources found at www.LysaTerKeurst.com.

Blog: Dialog with Lysa through her daily blog, see pictures of her family, and follow her speaking schedule. She'd love to meet you at an event in your area! Check out her blog at www.LysaTerKeurst.com.

Booking Lysa to speak: If you are interested in booking Lysa for a speaking engagement, contact Holly Goode at Holly@Proverbs31.org.

ABOUT PROVERBS 31 MINISTRIES

If you were inspired by *What Happens When Women Say Yes to God* and yearn to deepen your personal relationship with Jesus Christ, I encourage you to connect with Proverbs 31 Ministries. Proverbs 31 Ministries exists to be a trusted friend who will take you by the hand and walk by your side, leading you one step closer to the heart of God through

- *Encouragement for Today*, free online daily devotions
- *The P31 Woman* monthly magazine
- Daily radio program

To learn more about Proverbs 31 Ministries or to inquire about having Lysa TerKeurst speak at your event, contact Holly Goode at Holly@Proverbs31.org or visit www.Proverbs31.org.

Proverbs 31 Ministries
616-G Matthews-Mint Hill Road
Matthews, NC 28105
www.Proverbs31.org

Great Harvest House Reading
by Lysa TerKeurst

AM I MESSING UP MY KIDS?

Overflowing with practical ideas, short Bible studies, and plenty of encouragement, this inspiring resource will help you to realize that—with God's wisdom and mercy—you can experience peace and satisfaction while raising your kids.

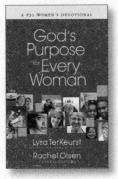

GOD'S PURPOSE FOR EVERY WOMAN

Proverbs 31 Ministry president Lysa TerKeurst and devotion coeditor Rachel Olson present this collection of heartfelt, insightful meditations selected to empower women to become fully devoted to God. Each day's offering includes a key Scripture, devotional, prayer, application steps, and reflection points verses to refresh and inspire you.

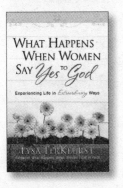

WHAT HAPPENS WHEN WOMEN SAY YES TO GOD

In *What Happens When Women Say Yes to God,* (a re-release of *Radically Obedient, Radically Blessed* with a new cover and updated material), Lysa shares inspiring stories from her own life along with compelling biblical insights as she describes the deep joy and great purpose of a life that honors God.

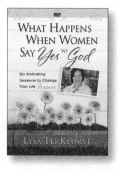

WHAT HAPPENS WHEN WOMEN SAY YES TO GOD DVD

In six powerful 30-minute sessions based on her popular book, Lysa inspires women to say "yes" to the remarkable path God has for them. Excellent for individuals or groups, this video series illuminates steps to a transforming faith. Includes helpful leader's guide.

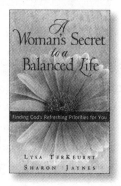

WHAT HAPPENS WHEN WOMEN WALK IN FAITH

Lysa continues to walk with you on your journey of faith in this follow-up book to *What Happens When Women Walk Say Yes to God.*

A WOMAN'S SECRET TO A BALANCED LIFE

From the leadership of Proverbs 31 Ministries comes this essential book, offering seven vital ways any Christian woman can prioritize her life more effectively. Cowritten with Sharon Jaynes.

Also by Lysa TerKeurst

Made to Crave

Made to Crave DVD Curriculum

and

Becoming More than a Good Bible Study Girl

Becoming More than a Good Bible Study Girl DVD Curriculum

Capture Her Heart (for husbands)

Capture His Heart (for wives)

Leading Women to the Heart of God

Living Life on Purpose

Who Holds the Key to Your Heart?